CONTENTS

1
STONE WORLD

Dr. STONE

1

STONE WORLD

STORY **RIICHIRO INAGAKI**
ART **BOICHI**

Dr. STONE

1

SHONEN JUMP Manga Edition

Story **RIICHIRO INAGAKI**
Art **BOICHI**

Translation/**CALEB COOK**
Touch-Up Art & Lettering/**STEPHEN DUTRO**
Design/**JULIAN [JR] ROBINSON**
Editor/**JOHN BAE**

Dr. STONE © 2017 by Riichiro Inagaki, Boichi
All rights reserved.
First published in Japan in 2017 by SHUEISHA Inc., Tokyo.
English translation rights arranged by SHUEISHA Inc.

Printed in the U.S.A.

Published by VIZ Media, LLC
P.O. Box 77010
San Francisco, CA 94107

10 9 8 7 6 5 4 3 2 1
First printing, September 2018

viz.com

shonenjump.com

BOICHI

Ah, so happy... Ahh, so very
happy... This book makes
me so happy!

This story's got everything!
Life in the great outdoors,
a postapocalyptic setting,
a scientist boy, primeval
visuals and characters with
the courage and conviction
not to yield to an unfamiliar
world. I seriously love it all,
and drawing it is super fun!

RIICHIRO INAGAKI

What do you imagine when
you think about scientists?
Glasses, introverts, maybe
a little mad...?

But in truth there can be
scientists who are charmers
and those who can be
muscly too.

Our protagonist, Senku, is
also be a bit different from
the scientists we're used to
imagining. He's one
hot-blooded guy!

Get ready to cheer for him
and his friends as they
face this unprecedented
challenge head-on!!

Boichi is a Korean-born artist
currently living and working in Japan.
His previous works include *Sun-Ken
Rock* and *Terra Formars Asimov*.

Riichiro Inagaki is a Japanese
manga writer from Tokyo. He is the
writer for the sports manga series
Eyeshield 21, which was serialized in
Weekly Shonen Jump.

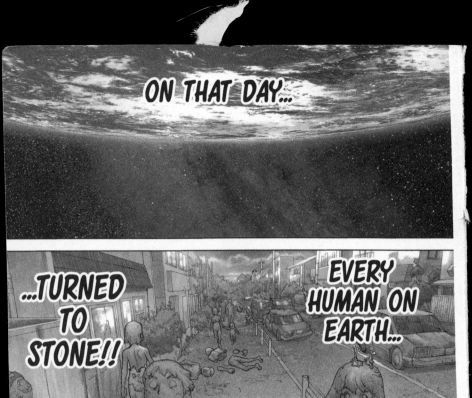

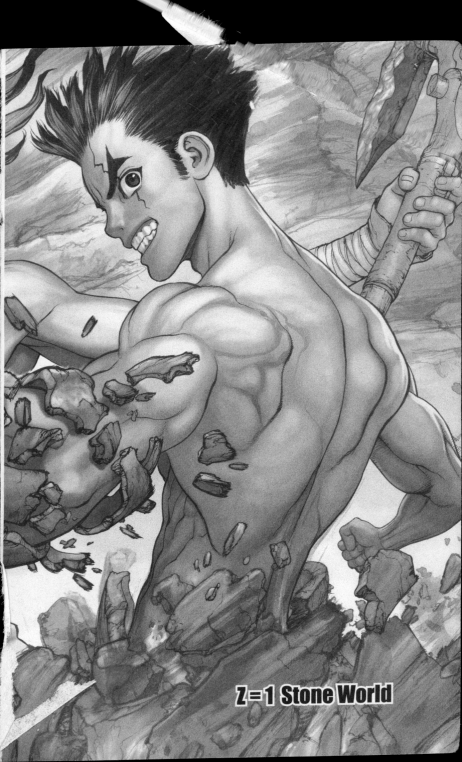

Z=1 Stone World

THANKS, SENKU, BUT...

...NO THANKS!

I CAN'T GO AND CHEAT MY WAY INTO HER HEART.

GLUG GLUG

...I TOLD YUZURIHA TO MEET ME UNDER THE CAMPHOR TREE.

THAT'S WHERE I'LL CONFESS!!

THAT'S RIGHT. LIKE THE HONEST AND UPRIGHT DUDE I AM...

REALLY?!

TEN THOUSAND YEN SAYS SHE'LL ACCEPT HIM, CONTRARY TO EXPECTATIONS.

FIVE HUNDRED SAYS SHE'LL REJECT HIM.

PUT ME DOWN FOR A HUNDRED.

I BET YOU 100 YEN THAT HE'LL GET TOTALLY REJECTED.

BUT TODAY'S THE DAY!

LISTEN TO ME, YUZURIHA!

THIS WHOLE TIME, I'VE BEEN TERRIFIED OF LOSING YUZURIHA AS A FRIEND!

?

...

THESE PAST FIVE YEARS, I'VE...

DESPITE THE POWERFUL NAME MY DEARLY DEPARTED PARENTS GAVE ME—TAIJU OKI—I'VE BEEN COWARDLY AND UNABLE TO FACE HER!

*TAIJU OKI MEANS "BIG-TREE BIG-TREE."

BUT...

I HAVE NO IDEA...

YUZU-RIHA!

HOLD ON TO THAT TREE!

<OH NO!>

<SLIPPING AWAY...>

<CONSCIOUS-NESS...>

<TERRORISTS? NO...>

<I CAN'T DIE YET. THERE'S STILL SO MUCH TO...>

IS
THIS...

DEATH?

MIGHT JUST BE THAT THIS POOR LITTLE BIRD IS SICK!

IT'S LIKE...THE SKIN AND FEATHERS GOT ALL HARD.

I'VE SEEN THIS BEFORE! A FRIEND OF MINE UPLOADED A PIC.

HAHH

HAHH

HAHH

Veterinary Clinic

OBVIOUSLY THE VET'S NOT GONNA BE OPEN BEFORE SCHOOL STARTS!

Clinic Hours:
10:00
10:30

...

Clinic Hours:
10:00~
10:30~

ANOTHER DUMMY WHO DOESN'T STOP TO THINK!

BECAUSE, WELL, HERE'S ANOTHER ONE!

NOW WE'RE BOTH GOING TO BE LATE FOR SCHOOL!

WHAT? STOP LAUGHING! WE'RE IN THE SAME BOAT, HERE!

Veterinary Clinic

WA HA HA HA!

WA HA HA HA HA HA!

YOU AIN'T WRONG ABOUT THAT!

NEVER.

WON'T
LET...

...MY
MIND
FADE.

HOW
MANY
YEARS
HAS IT
BEEN?

SINCE
THAT DAY...

NO! NO
MATTER
HOW
LONG...

I WON'T
LOSE THIS
FIGHT!

HOW MANY
DECADES?

HOW MANY
CENTURIES?

HOW
MANY
MILLENNIA?

CHIRP

CHIRP

IT'S BEEN
SEVERAL
THOUSAND
YEARS...

Z=1 STONE WORLD

...SINCE HUMANITY VANISHED FROM THE FACE OF THE EARTH.

I'M OUT!!

I'M FINALLY OUT!!

...FRAG- MENTS...?

STONE ...

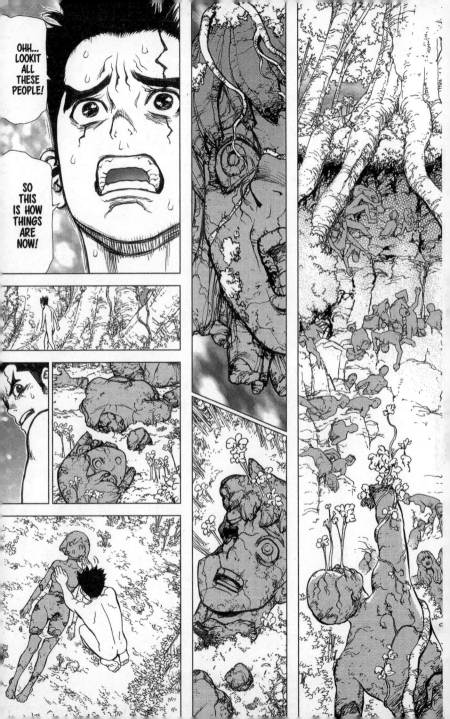

YUZURIHA.

EVER SINCE THAT DAY.

THIS WHOLE TIME...!

YOU SURVIVED.

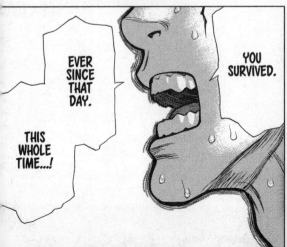

THERE'S NO MISTAKE...

EVEN AFTER ALL THESE MILLENNIA...

I'VE LOVED YOU.

FOR HUNDREDS...

...AND THOUSANDS OF YEARS!

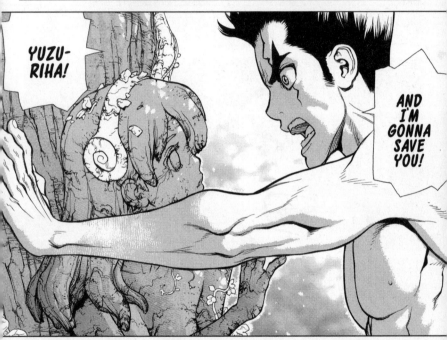

YUZU-RIHA!

AND I'M GONNA SAVE YOU!

HEAD DOWN THE RIVER, BIG ONE.

NOT SURE YET! BUT I'LL FIGURE IT OUT...

AS FOR HOW...

UH...

OHHHH!

DON'T YOU DARE HUG ME ALL NAKED LIKE THAT! I'LL KILL YOU!

TOMP TOMP TOMP

I'M...! I'M SO...

YOU SURVIVED, SENKU!!

HOW DO YOU KNOW...

...

TODAY IS OCTOBER 5, 5738.

YOU REALLY OVERSLEPT, YOU BIG JERK.

$E=mc^2$

I'VE BEEN UP AND WORKING FOR OVER HALF A YEAR NOW.

...THE EXACT DATE?

HUH?

...EMERGING IN WINTER BARE NAKED AND WITHOUT FOOD WOULD MEAN AN INSTANT GAME OVER.

I KNEW THAT IF I COULD, AT SOME POINT, WILL MYSELF TO AWAKEN...

IN THE DARKNESS?

SURVIVAL DEPENDED ON MAKING MY START IN SPRING.

THAT'S WHY KEEPING AN ACCURATE CALENDAR WAS AN ABSOLUTE NECESSITY.

THIS WHOLE TIME?

FOR REAL?

SENKU... YOU...

YOU DID ALL THIS YOURSELF?!

LOOK. WE'RE HERE.

ENOUGH CHATTER. TIME TO GET TO WORK.

FLIK

...TO ME!

SO JUST LEAVE THE HEAVY LIFTING...

THINKING AND BRAINPOWER...

...IS YOUR DEPARTMENT, SENKU!

WE'RE TAKING BACK THIS WORLD, YOU AND I!

WE'RE GONNA JUMP-START THAT PROCESS.

TRANSITIONING FROM THE STONE AGE TO MODERN CIVILIZATION TOOK HUMANITY...

...ABOUT TWO MILLION YEARS.

WE'LL ALSO USE THE POWER OF SCIENCE TO FIGURE OUT WHAT CAUSED THE PETRIFICATION AND OUR SUBSEQUENT REVIVAL.

WE MIGHT JUST BE A PAIR OF HIGH SCHOOL KIDS... ...BUT WE'RE GONNA CREATE CIVILIZATION FROM SCRATCH.

AND THEN...

...WE'LL SAVE YUZURIHA!!

Z=2: Fantasy vs. Science

MUGWORT! FOOD!

WHITE BEECHES! FOOD!

AMANITA MUSCARIA! POISONOUS!

YOU CAN TELL THEY'RE BAD NEWS BY HOW THEY LOOK. THEY'RE MARIO MUSHROOM LOOK-ALIKES!

AMANITA VIROSA! POISONOUS!

WOLF'S BANE! YOU TRYING TO KILL ME, FOOL?

ALSO, SALT ACTS AS A GREAT PRESERVATIVE FOR FOOD.

IT WAS PRIMEVAL MAN'S GREATEST DISCOVERY.

JUST SALT EXTRACTED FROM SEAWATER.

PEOPLE CAN EAT JUST ABOUT ANYTHING IF IT'S SALTED.

WHAT'D YOU SEASON THIS WITH?!

TASTYYYY!!

WOOO! OFF TO SEARCH IN THE OTHER DIRECTION!!

I MIGHT NOT BE GOOD AT CREATIVE THINKING, BUT...

...I'LL MAKE UP FOR IT WITH SPIRIT AND EFFORT!

NOM

NOM

THANKS, SENKU, FOR PRETTY MUCH EVERY-THING!

NEVER GONNA KNOW BY WONDERING. JUST GOTTA TRY!

POP

WILD GRAPES?

CAN I EAT 'EM?

ISN'T THIS WHERE I WAS FOR THOUSANDS OF YEARS?

THAT CAVE...

PLIP

PLIP

!

PLIP

PLIP

WHAT'S...

THIS?!

SOMEONE MUST'VE LEFT THIS HERE!

THERE MUST BE OTHER SURVIVORS BESIDES ME AND SENKU!!

IT WAS ME, FOOL.

YOU?!

LOOK. SEE THAT DRIPPING?

IT'S A MIRACULOUS LIQUID, CREATED BY THE BATS' GUANO.

NITRIC ACID!

I THOUGHT AS MUCH, YOU BIG OAF.

WUZZAT?!

SORRY, SENKU, I STILL DON'T GET IT!!

EXPLAINING IN DETAIL WOULD BE A PAIN, SO I WON'T.

DID YOU SAY NITRIC ACID?!

SO...YOU POUR THIS WHATCHA-MACALLIT ACID ON THERE...

...AND THE STONE ROTS AWAY, REVIVING THE BIRD, RIGHT?

IF ONLY IT WERE THAT SIMPLE.

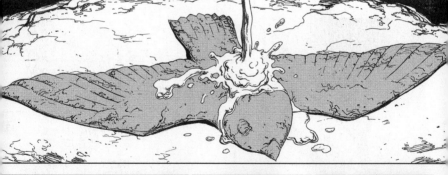

LABORATORY

I'VE ALREADY TRIED THIS A CRAZY NUMBER OF TIMES...

...WITH DIFFERENT METHODS AND DIFFERENT FACTORS.

...

...

IF WE ONLY HAD SOME BOOZE...

HEH HEH... THAT'S SO CLICHÉ.

SCIENCE DEMANDS DILIGENCE.

THIS IS WHY WE FORM HYPOTHESES AND PERFORM EXPERIMENTS!

...THAT EVEN SCIENCE CAN'T EXPLAIN...?

YOU MEAN THERE ARE SOME THINGS...

...WITH THE NITRIC ACID...

...TO PRODUCE A LIQUID KNOWN AS NITAL.

IT'S AN INDUSTRIAL-STRENGTH CORROSIVE AGENT.

WE COULD COMBINE THE ALCOHOL, OR ETHANOL...

"IF WE ONLY HAD SOME BOOZE."

OH? ABOUT THE NITAL? IT REVEALS THE GRAIN BOUNDARY OF FERRITES AND—

NOT THAT PART! I DON'T UNDERSTAND ALL THAT MUMBO JUMBO!

ABOUT WHAT YOU SAID JUST NOW...

HEY, SENKU...

THREE WEEKS.

JUST ABOUT TIME.

GULP

SIP

HOW TO MAKE WINE

Anyone can do it.

DON'T PUT A CAP ON

STIR DAILY

JUST SMASH SOME GRAPES AND RAISINS, PUT THEM IN A BOTTLE AND YOU'RE DONE!

HEH HEH... MAKING MOONSHINE IS ILLEGAL, THOUGH!!

IT'S REALLY WINE! WHO KNEW IT WOULD BE THIS EASY TO MAKE WITH JUST A FEW GRAPES...!

BLRF

OH! BETTER THAN I IMAGINED.

IT'S STILL TEN BILLION TIMES WORSE THAN THE WORST MASS-PRODUCED WINE.

$E=mc^2$

STEP BY STEP, DILIGENTLY!

KRACK KRACK

THIS NEXT PART IS GONNA BE A LITTLE MORE TEDIOUS...

AN INTRODUCTION TO DISTILLING WINE INTO BRANDY!!

NOTHING LEFT TO DO BUT TO DO IT!

I CAN'T WAIT!!

...CREATED CERAMICS LIKE THIS.

BEHOLD! EVEN THE MESOPOTAMIAN CIVILIZATIONS OF 3,000 B.C....

I DON'T GET IT!!

WHAT'S "DISTILLING"?

LABORATORY

BY HEATING, COOLING AND LETTING THE WINE CONDENSE, WE RAISE THE RELATIVE ALCOHOL CONTENT.

I THOUGHT AS MUCH.

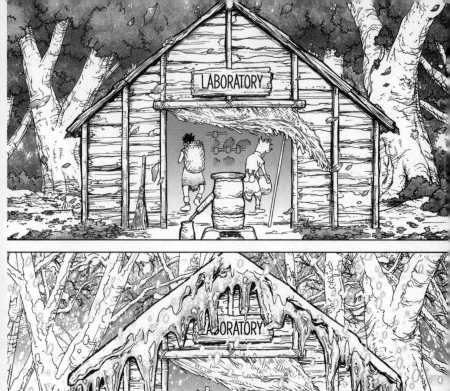

WE SHOULD PROBABLY DO SOMETHING ABOUT IT FOR PURELY HYGIENIC REASONS.

GETTING SICK OUT HERE WOULD BE GAME OVER.

YUZURIHA...

...IS GONNA HATE THIS!

SMELLS

THROB
THROB

FWIP

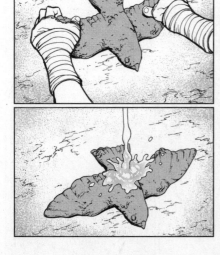

E=mc²

THE ANSWER...

...IS WAY OBVIOUS!!

TAIJU. THE GRAPES WERE YOUR IDEA TO BEGIN WITH...

...SO YOU GET TO DECIDE WHOM WE SAVE FIRST.

THANKS, SENKU!

...SINCE HUMANITY TURNED TO STONE!

IT'S BEEN SEVERAL MILLENNIA...

...AND TAIJU.

ONLY TWO HIGH SCHOOL BOYS MANAGED TO SURVIVE.

SENKU...

THEIR EFFORTS AND THE POWER OF SCIENCE HAVE YIELDED A FLUID THAT REVIVES THE PETRIFIED...!!

THEY'VE SPENT A YEAR SO FAR TRYING TO RESTART CIVILIZATION FROM SCRATCH!

Z=3: King of the Stone World

...TURNED BACK INTO DEAD FLESH.

IN MY TESTING, EVEN BROKEN PIECES OF STONE...

...AND THEN YUZURIHA'LL COME BACK TO LIFE, RIGHT?!

ALL WE NEED TO DO IS POUR THIS ON HER...

!!

YOU SICKO!

RIGHT!

MAY THEIR SOULS REST IN PEACE!

THOSE WERE INVALUABLE SACRIFICES, SO SAY A PRAYER FOR THEM.

I ALSO TRIED STICKING THE PIECES BACK TOGETHER BEFORE ADMINISTERING THE CURE.

BUT, ALAS, SOMETHING THAT'S ALREADY DEAD CAN'T BE REVIVED.

SORRY TO MAKE YOU WAIT 3,700 YEARS, YUZURIHA.

SPLSH

YUZURIHA ... ...IS NAKED!!

WE CAN'T REVIVE HER LIKE THIS!

WHO CAAAARES ABOUT CRAP LIKE THAT? WE LIVE IN A BRUTAL STONE WORLD NOW!!

REALLY, MORE IRRATIONAL NONSENSE OUTTA YOU?

NOBODY'S GONNA MIND SEEING A BARE BUTT OR SOMEONE'S JUNK SWINGING AROUND!

WHO CARES? I CARE!

Z=3: King of the Stone World

WHY HAVEN'T THE LIONS ACTUALLY ATTACKED US YET?

RIGHT! CUZ THERE'RE NO MORE HUMANS AROUND...

!

HEH HEH HEH... THINK ABOUT IT. TO THEM...

...WE'RE A COUPLE OF WEIRD BIPEDAL CREATURES THEY'VE NEVER SEEN BEFORE.

$E = mc^2$

HAHH

HAHH

HAHH

THIS GAME WAS STACKED AGAINST US FROM THE VERY START...!

OUR ONLY HOPE ARE THE SPEARS AND SHIELDS BACK AT CAMP...

...BUT THAT'S A CRAZY-FAR DISTANCE TO RUN.

THEY'RE BEING CAUTIOUS.

BUT IT'S STILL JUST A MATTER OF TIME.

...

UGH!

94

FSSHH FSSHH

AND I CAN MAKE YOU ONE PROMISE!

YOU TWO WILL NEVER BE IN DANGER AGAIN.

I'M READY FOR A FULL EXPLANA-TION.

TAKE IT NICE AND SLOW!

BRAINS! BRAWN! FISTS! THE THREE MUSKETEERS...

NOW HUMANITY'S GOT...

THIS IS GREAT, SENKU!

OHHHHHHH!

OH...

...ARE ON THE SCENE!!

...THIS GUY IS WAY TOO STRONG.

ALTHOUGH WITH MUSKETS NOT HAVING BEEN REINVENTED YET...

HEH HEH HEH... I SUPPOSE YOU'RE RIGHT.

THIS TSUKASA SHISHIO.

BAMMM

WHOAAA!!

Z=4: Pure White Seashells

WHAT'S WRONG WITH BEING TOO STRONG?

IT JUST MAKES HIM MORE RELIABLE!

IN THIS WORLD WITHOUT GUNS, THERE'S A TEN BILLION PERCENT CHANCE WE'D HAVE NO WAY OF STOPPING HIM.

OH, THAT'D BE BAD.

IN THAT CASE, I'D...

GET OVER HERE, YUZURIHA!

WE'RE TALKING ABOUT A GUY STRONG ENOUGH TO KILL A LION BAREHANDED, LIKE HE'S USING CHEAT CODES.

BUT WHAT IF...

...HE TURNS INTO AN EVIL, SEX-CRAZED TYRANT?

YOU'RE GONNA EAT THE LION?

IS IT EDIBLE?!

CAN I BORROW SOMETHING TO CUT FLESH?

A KNIFE, OR EVEN A STONE TOOL?

WHAT KINDA HIGH SCHOOLER WERE YOU?!

WHAT? YOU'VE EATEN LION BEFORE, SENKU?

YES, WHEN I TRAVELED TO AFRICA TO STUDY EBOLA.

THEY'RE NOT POISONOUS.

BUT THE MEAT'S TOUGH AND REEKS OF AMMONIA. IT'S SO NASTY YOU'D WANNA DIE.

EVEN IF I DID IT TO SAVE US, I STILL KILLED THIS BEAST.

THAT'S ALL IT IS.

...I'LL SHOW MY GRATITUDE TO THE CIRCLE OF LIFE.

YES...BY MAKING USE OF ITS REMAINS...

Z=4: Pure White Seashells

WITH SENKU AND ME WORKING TOGETHER... ...WE'LL BE FLUSH WITH PRESERVED FOOD.

WE HAVEN'T EVEN TAKEN A STEP YET?!

YUP. NOW WE CAN MOVE ON TO THE FIRST STEP TOWARD CIVILIZATION.

I GET IT. GRILL 'EM RIGHT AFTER CATCHING 'EM SO THEY DON'T GO ROTTEN, EVEN WITHOUT A FRIDGE!!

TO PUT IT IN A WAY EVEN YOUR WEAK MIND COULD UNDERSTAND, WE'RE SMOKING THEM.

NOT GRILLING. THE ALDEHYDES IN THE SMOKE ARE KILLING OFF ANY BACTERIA.

CORRECT ANSWER GETS TEN BILLION POINTS.

...WHEN BUILDING A SCIENTIFIC CIVILIZATION FROM SCRATCH?

WHAT'S THE FIRST AND MOST IMPORTANT THING...

TIME FOR A FUN LITTLE POP QUIZ.

YOUR UNBELIEVABLY STUPID ANSWER TURNED THE ALREADY LILY-WHITE TSUKASA SEVERAL SHADES PALER.

IF ONLY WE COULD WARP A FEW MILLION YEARS INTO THE FUTURE, BIG OAF!

THAT'D BE NICE! I'D KILL FOR A SMART-PHONE, YEAH!

SMART-PHONES?!

FIRST THING

SCIENTIFIC CIVILIZATION

MOST IMPORTANT THING

CALCIUM CARBONATE.

IS IT... IRON?

THERE'S SOMETHING EVEN HANDIER IN THE MEANTIME.

IRON WOULD BE GOOD TOO, BUT THAT'S A WAYS OFF.

SPLASH

SPLASH

THINK OF THE WHITE LINES DRAWN ACROSS SPORTING GROUNDS.

HOW CAN I PUT THIS SO EVEN OUR WEAK-MINDED MEMBER WILL GET IT?

YOU MEAN LIME?

OF COURSE! GIMME AN EXAMPLE AND...I PROBABLY STILL WON'T UNDERSTAND!

REMEMBER WHEN WE USED THESE SEASHELLS TO SHAVE YOUR BEARD, BIG OAF?

YES, AN EQUIPMENT SHED, OF COURSE!

...WE JUST GOTTA SEARCH IN A GYM EQUIPMENT SHED?

SO TO GET OUR HANDS ON SOME OF THIS CALCIUM-THINGY...

BY SMASHING THEM INTO A FINE POWDER...

...

IN A WORLD 3,700 YEARS POST-CIVILIZATION!

IF ONLY THOSE STILL EXISTED!

...YOU REMAINED CALM AND GAVE ME AN INSTANT SUMMARY OF OUR SITUATION.

JUST AFTER REVIVING ME, DURING THE FIGHT WITH THE LIONS...

...AN INCREDIBLE MAN.

SENKU, YOU ARE...

I'VE NEVER MET ANYONE QUITE AS CAPABLE AS YOU.

YOU HAVE MY DEEPEST RESPECT.

WHAT'RE YOU REALLY TRYING TO SAY?

...IS EITHER FLIRTING OR SCHEMING.

A MAN WHO'D PRAISE ANOTHER MAN TO HIS FACE...

YEAH.

THAT'S ALL I WAS THINKING, REALLY.

...CREATE MODERN CIVILIZATION FROM NOTHING.

I'M CONVINCED THAT YOU'LL REALLY BE ABLE TO...

DON'T BE LIKE THAT. I DIDN'T MEAN ANYTHING MORE BY IT.

THWUMP

SO! WHAT'S NUMBER FOUR?

THE FOURTH IMPORTANT USE FOR THESE SEASHELLS.

YOU SAID THERE WERE FOUR OF THEM, RIGHT?

GUESS A BAD MEMORY'S PART OF MY WEAK MIND!!

WA HA HA HA! IS THAT RIGHT?

...?

NO. JUST THREE.

DIDN'T I SAY THREE?

$E=mc^2$

SPLASH

SHELLS!

SHELLS!

SHELLS!

SPLASH

...IS SO FREE.

THIS STONE WORLD OF OURS...

NOT THE SEA. NOT THE LAND...

LIKE THESE SHELLS. THEY NEVER BELONGED TO ANYONE.

...FOR HIS AILING SISTER.

THE SISTER LOVED TALES OF MERMAID PRINCESSES, YOU SEE.

LONG AGO, THERE WAS A POOR BOY.

HE WANTED TO MAKE A NECKLACE OF SHELLS...

HE REEKED OF BOOZE.

A MAN WITH A SO-CALLED FISHING LICENSE, ABOUT THE SAME AGE AS THIS STONE MAN HERE.

ONE DAY, A MIDDLE-AGED MAN APPEARED BEFORE HIM.

IN THE END, THE BOY WAS NEVER ABLE...

...TO MAKE HIS LITTLE SISTER A MERMAID PRINCESS...

THE BOY WAS BEATEN TO THE POINT OF DISFIGURE-MENT.

ACCORDING TO THE MAN...

COLLECTING THOSE SEASHELLS AMOUNTED TO STEALING.

YOU KNOW WHAT YOU JUST DID, YEAH?

TSUKASA. THAT RIGHT THERE...

...WAS A HUMAN YOU JUST KILLED.

TUMP

TUMP

BUT ONCE CIVILIZATION IS UP AND RUNNING...

NO DOUBT THEY'LL BE BEYOND GRATEFUL AT FIRST.

THE POOR AND WEAK WILL BE VICTIMIZED ALL OVER AGAIN.

I CAN'T LET THAT HAPPEN.

...THEY'LL SAY, "THAT'S MY LAND." "PAY ME RENT AND TAXES."

SENKU. DOES YOUR PLAN TO SAVE EVERYONE INCLUDE...

I'M WELL AWARE.

...EVERY BLACK-HEARTED ADULT?

BUT THE LIONS WOULD'VE WIPED US OUT IF WE HADN'T WOKEN TSUKASA.

WE REALLY DIDN'T HAVE A CHOICE.

AN EVIL DICTATOR WOULD'VE BEEN TEN BILLION TIMES BETTER THAN THIS.

HEH HEH HEH... THIS GUY'S SERIOUSLY BAD NEWS.

TMP

THE CAVE AND ITS MIRACLE FLUID...

...I'LL KEEP THEM HIDDEN FROM TSUKASA OR DIE TRYING!

LOOKIE, SENKU, TSUKASA!

THAT SECRET IS OUR TRUMP CARD AGAINST TSUKASA.

HE WANTS TO SAVE ONLY YOUNG PEOPLE?

I'D BETTER NOT DO ANYTHING CRAZY, LIKE LETTING HIM FIGURE OUT THE REVIVAL FLUID FORMULA.

TOMP TOMP TOMP TOMP TOMP TOMP TOMP

I'VE GOT ENOUGH MIRACLE FLUID FROM THE CAVE!

For Yuzuriha

WE CAN SAVE YUZURIHA FOR REAL THIS TIME!!

Z=5: Yuzuriha

For Yuzuriha

WHAT?! I JUMPED THE GUN? SORRY, I'LL RUN AND GET SOME MORE!!

...FLUID TO REVIVE A SINGLE PERSON.

WHAT THE HECK? WE DON'T HAVE QUITE ENOUGH...

ALL RIGHT, YUZURIHA!

...WHILE YOU DASH OVER THERE, BIG OAF.

TSUKASA AND I CAN WAIT HERE AND PLAY 20 QUESTIONS...

THIS TIME WE'RE GONNA SAVE YOU FOR REAL!

SHF

I'M THE QUICKEST, SO I SHOULD GO.

WHY DON'T YOU TELL ME...

...WHERE TO FIND THIS MIRACLE FLUID?

...THERE'S A TEN BILLION PERCENT CHANCE OF STOPPING MY PLAN TO REVIVE ALL OF HUMANITY!

BECAUSE IF HE CAN COMMANDEER THE SOURCE OF THE FLUID...

HEH HEH HEH... TOO EASY. HE TOOK THE BAIT.

WHOOSH

IT STAINS MY SKIN YELLOW?

BATS...

I SEE. THE MIRACLE FLUID...

...IS NITRIC ACID.

GOOD POINT!

BUT THEN, WHY'D YOU SEND TSUKASA AWAY?!

DIDN'T YOU SAY WE DIDN'T HAVE ENOUGH FLUID?

WHY WOULD I PUT A POT IN THE CAVE THAT'S THE WRONG SIZE?

WHAT'S GOING ON, SENKU?!

TSUKASA'S A GOOD GUY!

GET RID OF HIM? WHY?

BECAUSE HE'S UNMANAGEABLE.

HE MIGHT KNOW THE CAVE'S LOCATION NOW, BUT...

...I NEEDED TO GET RID OF HIM BEFORE WE REVIVED YUZURIHA.

IT WAS SOME DOUBLE-EDGED BAIT.

HEH HEH HEH... A COMPETITION TO RESTART CIVILIZATION? I CAN'T WAIT.

I DON'T HAVE EVEN ONE MILLIMETER OF INTEREST IN A SO-CALLED STRONGEST WORLD BUILT IN HIS IMAGE.

WE'LL LIVE AMONG NATURE, WHERE NO ONE CAN LAY CLAIM TO ANYTHING.

WE SHOULD ONLY REVIVE THE PURE-HEARTED YOUTH.

YEAH.

TSUKASA SHISHIO IS...

SOMETHING HAPPENED...

...WHILE I WAS GONE, RIGHT?!

GOT IT! NO EXPLANATION NEEDED.

IF THAT'S WHAT YOU SAY, SENKU, THEN THAT'S HOW IT IS.

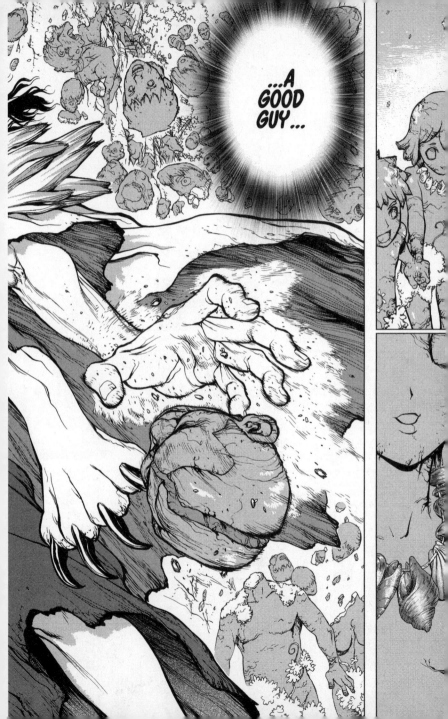

...A GOOD GUY...

IT RESEMBLES COLD SLEEP.

STOP PANICKING. THE REACTION TAKES TIME.

DON'T WORRY, YUZU-RIHA!

WE SHOULDN'T WORRY, RIGHT?!

...

NOTHING'S HAPPEN-ING!

TOO COMPLICATED! I'M TOTALLY LOST!

IT'S JUST A THEORY I'VE COOKED UP BASED ON A YEAR'S WORTH OF EXPERIMENTS.

SOME MYSTERY ELEMENT TRIGGERED THE PHASE CHANGE, PRESERVING THE STONE STATE.

IT'S LIKE A PROTECTIVE LAYER MADE UP OF TRACE METALS IN THE BODY.

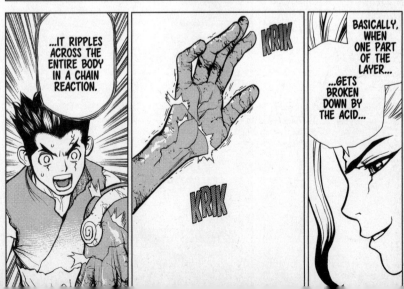

...IT RIPPLES ACROSS THE ENTIRE BODY IN A CHAIN REACTION.

KRIK

KRIK

BASICALLY, WHEN ONE PART OF THE LAYER...

...GETS BROKEN DOWN BY THE ACID...

UNDOING...

...THE PETRIFI-CATION!

LISTEN TO ME, YUZURIHA!

THESE PAST FIVE YEARS, I'VE...

I HAVE TO!!

I'LL CONFESS.

I WON'T DIE.

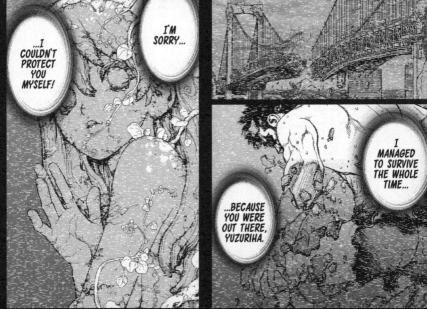

...I COULDN'T PROTECT YOU MYSELF!

I'M SORRY...

I MANAGED TO SURVIVE THE WHOLE TIME...

...BECAUSE YOU WERE OUT THERE, YUZURIHA.

WE ONLY HAVE TWO OPTIONS, SO CHOOSE!

HE SPENT A YEAR COMING UP WITH THE REVIVAL FLUID...

ITS ALL THANKS TO SENKU, REALLY.

...WE NEED TO MAKE A QUICK DECISION BEFORE TSUKASA RETURNS!

HEH HEH HEH... TERRIBLY SORRY TO CUT THIS LITTLE REUNION SHORT, BUT...

...RUN AWAY RIGHT NOW.

LIVE OUT YOUR LIVES SOMEWHERE FAR AWAY.

TAIJU AND YUZURIHA, YOU TWO...

PLAN A!

PLAN B!

WE FIGHT...

...WITH THE TOOLS OF CIVILIZATION!

WE ALL FIGHT TO PUT A STOP TO THAT MURDERER, TSUKASA.

Dr.STONE

YOU TWO EITHER RUN AWAY RIGHT NOW...

...OR WE ALL STAND AND FACE TSUKASA TOGETHER!

Z=6: Taiju vs. Tsukasa

THE ANSWER'S OBVIOUS!

BAM

IF TSUKASA IS RUNNING AROUND SMASHING STONE PEOPLE...

...THEN I'VE GOT NO CHOICE BUT TO...

IF HE'S REALLY KILLING THEM LIKE THAT...

UH-HUH... STILL NOT SURE WHAT'S HAPPENING, BUT I'LL DO WHATEVER I CAN TO HELP!

NOD NOD NOD

NOD

GOOD TO SEE YOU'RE BOTH FIRED UP AND IN SYNC, BUT YOU NEED TO LISTEN TO ME, YOU OLD COUPLE.

I DIDN'T MAKE THE SUGGESTION OUT OF KINDNESS. RUNNING MAY BE THE MOST RATIONAL CHOICE IN THIS CASE.

OF COURSE WE STAND AND FIGHT, DUH!

DON'T MISJUDGE ME AND YUZURIHA LIKE THAT, SENKU.

Z=6: Taiju vs. Tsukasa

IF SOMETHING HAPPENS TO ME, TAKE CARE OF YUZURIHA.

SENKU.

...GONNA STOP TSUKASA!

I'M...

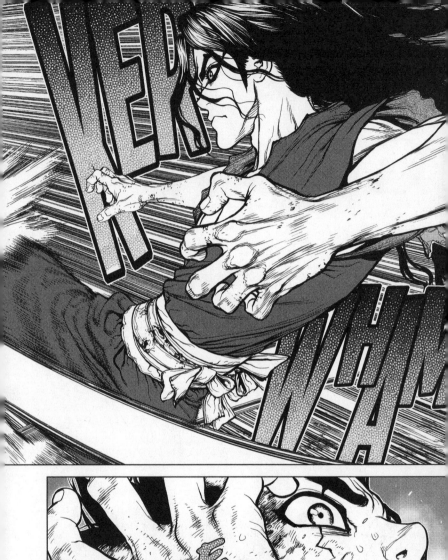
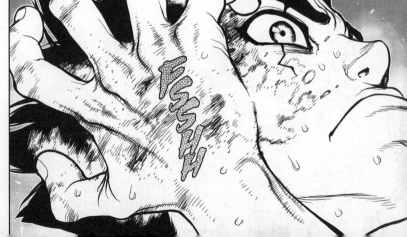

SKFSKFSKFSKF

WHY NOT?

IT'S NOT AS IF YOU COULDN'T ATTACK JUST NOW.

YOU JUST DIDN'T WANT TO...

...AFTER TAKING ONE OF MY KICKS.

MORE IMPORTANTLY...

YOU'RE THE FIRST TO EVER STAY UPRIGHT...

BUT YOU CAN PUNCH AND KICK ME ALL YOU LIKE.

I DON'T HIT PEOPLE!

KILLING PEOPLE LIKE THAT IS WRONG!!

IN RETURN, AGREE TO STOP SMASHING THOSE STATUES, TSUKASA!

LET ME MAKE SURE I UNDERSTAND YOU.

TAIJU...

YEAH, EXACTLY!!

IS THAT IT?

YOU'RE SAYING I CAN KEEP HITTING YOU...

...INSTEAD OF DESTROYING THE STATUES?

HOW'S THAT A DEAL?

I DON'T GET IT.

THEN... THE GIRL YOU JUST REVIVED...

ATTACK ALL YOU WANT! I'LL NEVER QUIT TRYING TO STOP YOU!!

IF YOU KEEP STANDING IN MY WAY...

BA M

RUNNING MAY BE THE MOST RATIONAL CHOICE IN THIS CASE.

I SEE. I'M BASICALLY A HOSTAGE NOW!

THAT'S WHAT SENKU MEANT...

HOW ABOUT I KILL YUZURIHA?

THERE'S ONLY ONE WAY LEFT TO STOP TSUKASA...

WE'LL HAVE TO TURN THE CLOCK FORWARD.

AND HE GRABBED IT.

LIKE "BAM"...

MY CROSSBOW FIRED THIS ARROW AT OVER 200 KM PER HOUR.

WHAT A MONSTER. HE'S VIRTUALLY INVINCIBLE, IN THIS AGE.

...HUMANITY'S GREATEST INVENTION.

IN ALL OF HISTORY...

I'M TALKING FIREARMS.

WRONG!

SMART-PHONES...?

YOU REALLY LIKE SMART-PHONES, HUH?

...GUNPOWDER IS OUR ONLY OPTION!

TO FIGHT AGAINST AN INVINCIBLE, MURDEROUS FIEND LIKE TSUKASA...

NOO, WHAT A WASTE!

WHAT'RE YOU DOING, SENKU??

I'M MAKING IT LOOK LIKE WE GRABBED ONLY THE FOOD AND RAN OFF IN FEAR OF TSUKASA.

JUST STAGING THE SCENE.

KRUKK

KRAK

Z=7: The Gunpowder Adventure

IF WE CAN GET OUR HANDS ON SOME GUNPOWDER, WE WIN!

BUT WE'RE SUNK IF TSUKASA FIGURES OUT OUR PLAN FIRST!

THAT'S THE KINDA RACE WE'RE IN NOW!

Z=7: The Gunpowder Adventure

HAKONE IS OUR DESTINATION!

THIS GRAND ADVENTURE OF OURS WILL ONLY TAKE US 80 KILOMETERS AWAY!

WE'RE OFF TO GET THE RAW MATERIALS FOR GUNPOWDER!!

KLIK

KLAK

A SEXTANT ALLOWS ONE TO DETERMINE GLOBAL POSITION BASED ON THE TIME, BUT THIS ONE'S SO INACCURATE IT'S BASICALLY TRASH.

YOU SAY THAT LIKE COUNTING THAT HIGH IS NO BIG DEAL?

IT'S BEEN 35,970 SECONDS SINCE THE SUN ROSE TODAY.

SENKU COUNTED TO 100 BILLION OR WHATEVER WHILE WE WERE STATUES. A FEW THOUSAND IS EASY AS PIE FOR HIM!

WUZZAT, SENKU?

A SEXTANT.

A LANDMARK IN KAMAKURA?

COME TO THINK OF IT...

HM... HOW ABOUT USING A BUILDING AS A LANDMARK?

ALL CONCRETE AND STEEL CRUMBLED AWAY. THERE'S NOTHING LEFT.

UNFORTUNATELY, THIS PIECE OF TRASH IS THE ONLY FORM OF GPS WE HAVE.

Sigh

IF ONLY I KNEW OUR EXACT CO-ORDINATES ...!

I THINK WE'RE NEAR KAMA-KURA...

...IN THAT SPOT OVER THERE?

WHY AREN'T THERE PLANTS GROWING...

HEH HEH HEH... I KNOW EXACTLY WHERE WE ARE.

WE'RE 35.19 DEGREES NORTH...

...BY 139.32 DEGREES EAST!

NO, I'M NOT CRYING!

!

WAS IT ME?

WELL, I MEAN, I AM, BUT NOT LIKE YOU THINK, TAIJU!

WHAT'S WRONG, YUZURIHA? WHERE'S THE JERK WHO MADE YOU CRY?

SEEING THE GREAT BUDDHA OF KAMAKURA...

...SO IT HASN'T REALLY HIT ME UNTIL NOW.

I ONLY JUST WOKE UP TODAY...

EITHER WAY, YOU GET WHAT I'M SAYING!

Or Buddha?

HE STOOD HERE FOR THOUSANDS OF YEARS, NEVER CORRODING AWAY! THANK GOD.

THE GREAT BUDDHA HERE SHOWED US THE WAY!

...WHOSE CHEMICAL COMPOSITION IS MORE RESISTANT TO CORROSION.

NO. IT'S STILL STANDING BECAUSE IT'S MADE OF BRONZE...

THE BIG GUY MADE IT EASIER FOR US TO FIND HIM!!

BUT LOOK! THERE'RE NO PLANTS SPROUTING AROUND THE GREAT BUDDHA!

THAT'S TOXIC FOR MOST VEGETATION.

NO. THE COPPER IONS JUST SEEPED INTO THE SOIL.

RESTING IS PART OF THE JOB, YOU BIG OAF.

GO TO BED, ALREADY.

LITER-ALLY!

JUST BARELY HAVE MY HEAD ABOVE WATER...

HEH HEH HEH... THAT BIG OLD BODY OF YOURS FINALLY BREAKING DOWN?

I STILL HAVE A LOT LEFT IN THE TANK, SO DON'T WORRY!

SENKU...

YOU'RE NOT THE KIND OF MAN TO RUN OFF WITH YOUR TAIL BETWEEN YOUR LEGS.

BY LOOKING AT ALL THESE JUMBLED FOOT-PRINTS...

...I CAN TELL THEY FLED IN A HURRY.

OR...SO THEY'D LIKE ME TO THINK.

BUT WHY?

BUT WHERE?

WITH A WEAPON.

IT'S OBVIOUS.

THEY MEAN TO FIGHT ME.

THEY'RE CREATING A SCIENTIFIC WEAPON.

AND NOW YOU'VE HEADED WEST FOR SOME UNKNOWN REASON?

LYING ABOUT TAIJU NEEDING DAYS OF REST...

OUR FIRST REAL BATH IN 3,700 YEARS!

THIS IS JUST THE THING TO SOOTHE A WEARY BODY!

HEH HEH HEH... WE DIDN'T COME HERE FOR THE SPA TREATMENT.

Ah...

Women

...THE RAW INGREDIENT FOR GUNPOWDER... SULFUR!

WE MIGHT AS WELL TAKE ADVANTAGE OF...

THANKFULLY, JAPAN IS A VOLCANIC NATION.

SO IF YOU'RE TAKING A TRIP TO THE HOT SPRINGS...

THEY MUST BE IN HAKONE!

IF THEY MAKE GUNPOWDER, I'LL BE AT THEIR MERCY.

Side Story
Let's Make Some Pottery!!

Ohh...

LEMME HELP MAKE SOME POTTERY!!

I CAN'T JUST LEAVE ALL THIS HARD WORK TO YOU, SENKU.

I'M KINDA CLUMSY, SO THIS WAY'S BETTER!

COIL METHOD FOR ME!

...OR BUILD UP LAYERS OF COILED CLAY.

YOU CAN EITHER USE A POTTER'S WHEEL...

YUZURIHA'S

SQUISH SQUISH

Side Story (End)

YOU'RE READING THE WRONG WAY

Dr. STONE
reads from right to left, starting in the upper-right corner. Japanese is read from right to left, meaning that action, sound effects and word-balloon order are completely reversed from English order.

Black ✦ Clover

STORY & ART BY YŪKI TABATA

Asta is a young boy who dreams of becoming the greatest mage in the kingdom. Only one problem—he can't use any magic! Luckily for Asta, he receives the incredibly rare five-leaf clover grimoire that gives him the power of anti-magic. Can someone who can't use magic really become the Wizard King? One thing's for sure—Asta will never give up!

SHONEN JUMP

VIZ media
www.viz.com